Thinking History
by **Peter N. Stearns**

A service of the American Historical Association's
Institutional Services Program

Peter N. Stearns is provost and professor of history at George Mason University.

Copyeditor: David Darlington

Layout and production: Chris Hale

Published in 2004 by the American Historical Association. As publisher, the American Historical Association does not adopt official views on any field of history and does not necessarily agree or disagree with the views expressed in this book.

ISBN: 0-87229-133-2

CONTENTS

Preface

Few students in the United States can escape several required history courses, from middle school through the early years of college. Some resent the requirements—in certain cases because the courses are badly taught, in others because it seems onerous to have to take a subject, in still others because the kind of thinking involved is simply not appealing. (One of my kids, now a scientist, never found history entirely appealing because it couldn't offer precise answers to big questions, precisely the reason I like it.) Nevertheless, many students, even in required settings, develop a "love" of history, and quite a few will take even more history courses than they are forced to do. And there are all sorts of gradations in between.

Unfortunately, the series of required history courses tends to obscure our ability to articulate why history should in fact be studied. Teachers don't have to debate the topic, since students have to take the courses anyway; and some teachers never develop the habit of thinking specifically about how they would define the history essentials. History textbooks usually have an introduction that talks a bit about why history should be studied, or at least why U.S. or world history should be studied. But the sections are short, not always well thought out, and rarely read (since they're rarely assigned). It's also true that some of the most common forms of history testing—common because they're inexpensive—don't really get at the main reasons for knowing history, which poses a real dilemma for the field.

Students in any subject should be encouraged to ask why they're studying it, and explore the main reasons for doing so. Required history courses are just as deficient in their lack of self-conscious justifications as required math or science courses. But science and math may at least seem more relevant in a modern, high-tech world than history. Historians often exacerbate this by skimping on basic issues in favor of all the history facts that good students should know. So there is reason to step back and ask, and try to answer, some of the big questions about what history learning is all about.

That is the purpose of this pamphlet, with its two related essays on how the purposes of history teaching and learning have evolved and why history should be studied. The goal is to open an explicit discussion, not to pretend that everyone agrees on all the answers. A good history course should allow recurrent opportunity to pull away from daily routines and talk about what's really important—the skills being learned and how history, in fact, relates to life after the classroom. Hopefully, the essays will encourage and inform this kind of every-so-often soul-searching.

The essays are designed, almost equally, for students who don't like history and for students who do. For students who don't, the essays try to explain why historical thinking is important, and why history does not really center on endless memorization of dead facts. The goal here is to persuade some of you that you don't have to dislike history after all. This is not a sterile plea: many students have passed from a dull history course to one that's analytically challenging and have changed their minds about the whole subject. But even for students who give these essays a chance and still don't "like" history, it will help to have some sense of what the subject is fundamentally about, and what can be gained from it.

The essays are equally important, I believe, for those who already like history. Many students find subjects appealing for reasons they can't quite put their finger on. Many history teachers, myself included, probably loved history long before they could fully articulate what the subject was about, or even why they liked it. This is compounded by the wide range of reasons one might enjoy a subject such as history, which makes it impossible to offer a simple or easy justification. Still, it is important, particularly when one does like a subject, to know its fundamental goals, and to be able to explain to others why the enthusiasm might be contagious. Again, the main point is to step back from the kind of detail that history courses—like any subject—usually have to grapple with, to talk about basic purposes and justifications.

History courses build knowledge that many people find relevant as measurements of successful education. They build skills, as well as knowledge, absolutely essential for citizenship. They build habits, perspectives and experiences also fundamental in a whole variety of professions, and make the panorama of life more interesting and meaningful. That's why some of us value history so much that we organize our lives around its exploration. That's why, more prosaically, some history courses are required. That's why it's important to be able to think about the relationship between history courses and these larger claims for meaning and significance. That's the relationship, finally, that history students and teachers need to be able to discuss, and that's what these essays are designed to encourage.

The History of History and What History Can Be

The human impulse to ponder the past runs very deep. The twin goals of most early history—which remain quite valid today—involved identity and understanding. Most early societies generated oral stories about the group's origins and some of the events that marked it. These were often myth or wishful thinking, but many picked up at least elements of the group's actual past. The earliest written story in the ancient Middle East, the epic of Gilgamesh, tells of a massive flood sent by the gods to punish man. While it undoubtedly embellished what really happened, it almost certainly picked up on a real catastrophe that people thought should be remembered, and conferred a special identity to the societies involved. Chinese authors probably mixed real memories and legend in writing about the first dynasties in China. These served as a source of Chinese identity and as a model for how Chinese institutions, and particularly the office of emperor, should be organized in imitation of their origins. Stories of the past also helped societies sort out family origins, or who belonged to whom, another source of identity. A key function of older people in many groups was to pass on detailed information of this sort.

Understanding involved looking at events of the past—sometimes the recent past—to help sort out why current patterns were as they were. Early Greek historians, particularly Thucydides writing of a major war between Athens and Sparta, used a commentary on the past to explain resultant conflicts and weaknesses in contemporary Greece. Sometimes, this attempt to record the past could become a mere list of happenings. During the Middle Ages, many monks in Christian Europe carefully chronicled events of each year, to create a record that would be remembered, one short entry after another. It is not always clear what purpose they thought they were fulfilling, though in fact their chronicles provided rich sources of information to later historians. Again, their effort shows the strong impulse to record and use the past in some fashion.

As history has evolved, and as it is used today, it embraces a number of purposes, building on the ideas of identity and understanding. Some of the purposes may have become a bit routine, but some involve a manner of thinking—thinking historically—that is a powerful tool for understanding the world we live in.

❖ History as Fact

History is a fact-based discipline, and there can be no historical thinking without knowing some facts—often, a lot of facts. To many history students and some teachers, history, when taught, can seem nothing but a parade of data, a list of one thing after another to learn. Though the method is less popular today, in the past students in some history classes had to learn all the kings of England, or all the American presidents, in order. Because history deals not only with facts but with sequences of time, chronological facts—dates—often seem very important, and these too must sometimes be memorized. As a result, historical intelligence can seem like a giant game of *Jeopardy*, a test of one's willingness to commit information to memory without much active thought. Because it is so easy to test factual knowledge in machine-gradable forms, assessing historical talents also, often, becomes a memorization exercise. This process delights some students, who enjoy definite data, but leaves many others thinking that history, as a subject, is rather bleak.

Self-styled experts can add to this sense, by producing lists of historical facts that every educated person ought to know. Several were produced in the 1980s, with a thousand facts every student should know about United States or world (mainly Western) history. Periodically, throughout the past century, similar experts have noted the huge gaps in the factual knowledge American students have about history, and have wondered what's the matter with the schools, or with modern youth. Memorized historical knowledge has often been used as a screening device, to separate the educated from the ignorant. Despite its persistence, this is not a very appealing aspect of the discipline.

❖ History as Narrative Storytelling

In truth, it's difficult to strike a proper balance. Factual ignorance—such as not knowing which came first, the American Revolution or the Civil War—is truly distressing to people who not only know the facts but think they're important, including of course many history teachers. Too much factual ignorance makes historical thinking impossible. But, increasingly, most history teachers argue that facts are building blocks, not ends in themselves, emphasizing the ability to use facts effectively to understand the past.

Finding more to do with historical facts than simply memorize them goes well back in many intellectual traditions, often in ways related to both identity and understanding. Many people are drawn to history as a source of powerful stories, which weave in facts but go beyond them to offer insights about human nature and the range of human capacity, for evil and for good. Biographies and military histories continue to be the most popular kinds of history in the United States today, measured in terms of book sales and television renditions. For many, well-told historical stories surpass fiction for drama, as the fact that they actually happened adds to the fascination.

By the time of the European Renaissance, history was seen as offering other forms of understanding—beyond facts and stories for their own sake that still resonate today. The central idea is that history provides a wealth of examples of human and social behavior, ranging well beyond what is available merely by examining and present and offering added benefits of perspective or hindsight. Many people have long believed that leaders could learn both morality and tactics by studying real-life dilemmas in the past, when choices had to be made about whether to sacrifice principle for the sake of personal or social gain. Machiavelli, the Italian political thinker who advocated pragmatic methods of keeping and retaining political power, used historical examples from Greece and Rome, as well as the more recent Italian past, to show latter-day rulers what would work and what would not. Similarly, students today could use historical stories to think about courage, and perhaps become more courageous in real life. History, in other words, can be seen as a great treasure house of examples, of what to do and what not to do, in various walks of life. It provides a focus for moral contemplation, as the phrase "history teaching by example" suggests. Many educators today still think of history—whether of "great men" or of ordinary people who provide lessons in protest or in overcoming great odds—as a means of providing models for aspiration and behavior. History thus serves as a key way to provide positive socialization for children en route to adulthood.

Historical episodes can serve a similar function in strategic training. Histories of battles can often drive home lessons about success or failure in war. The assumption is twofold: first, that the real examples of history are more compelling than imaginary exercises; and second, that historical patterns may repeat themselves, so that learning what succeeded or failed in the past provides active guidance for the future. Even today, America's military academies offer far more training in ancient history than most college history departments, primarily because ancient battles (juxtaposed with modern examples) seem to present particularly useful lessons in military strategy. In the absence of a real-life laboratory, history provides some sense of what people will do in various situations, and what might have to be done in the future.

The belief in the past as a laboratory for possibly recurring or recycling human experiences lies behind the common phrase (from the philosopher Santayana), that "those who do not know the past are condemned to repeat it." This assumes that individuals and societies can learn from past mistakes, but if they are stubbornly ignorant of the past the mistakes will be repeated.

A classic modern example of this kind of thinking about history and its uses involves what is often called the Munich analogy. In 1938, the leaders of Britain and France met with Hitler, who had just invaded parts of Czechoslovakia. Rather than threatening force against this aggression, they hoped the conciliation would work, and easily believed Hitler's assurances that his appetites were quenched. The British leader came back from the Munich conference claiming he had obtained "peace in our time." In fact, within months Hitler was on the march again, convinced by Munich that the British and French would do nothing to counter further aggression, while the British and French found their reactions hampered by the illusions of Munich. Munich's failure, according to many historians and leaders alike, demonstrates the importance of a firm stance against aggressors—for to do otherwise would be to fail to learn from one of the great lessons of recent history. The Munich analogy—the belief that various subsequent situations were essentially the same as Munich, where appeasement would simply lead to further aggression—powerfully affected American policy decisions in the Cold War, particularly in Korea and Vietnam. And analogy continues to operate, particularly in diplomatic and military thinking. Many American leaders, from 1990 to 2003, repeatedly compared Iraqi leader Saddam Hussein to Hitler, convinced that the association would increase world condemnation of Saddam but also that it should guide a policy of preemptive action against an evil aggressor.

While historians are always pleased that people find history useful, many warn against facile equations or analogies with the past. They argue that situations vary too much for analogies to be all that informative—in fact, sometimes they vary so much that analogies are positively harmful. They note that Vietnamese communists were not in fact Hitler, bent on expansion at all costs, and that analogies with Munich made the United States too ready to get involved in what turned out to be a very complicated conflict. The cautions about analogy still require knowledge of history, however, to help determine what popular equations with the past may be misleading and why. Obviously these cautions lack the ready appeal of the sense that history can directly guide policy in the future. We'll have to come back to the analogy dilemma when we talk about historical thinking in general.

❖ History as a Moral and Strategic Example

History as moral and strategic example sustained a good bit of historical teaching and writing in Western civilization from the Renaissance to the 18th century. It seemed particularly important to offer history to future leaders, to society's elite, who would really need this kind of guidance and whose historical knowledge—particularly of Greece and Rome—would further distinguish them from ordinary folks. And we have seen that these basic arguments for the need to know history still continue powerfully today. The 19th century added another component to the argument for history, around an updated version of the need for identity. History was targeted at everyone, not just the elite. The 19th and 20th centuries were the great age of nationalism, first in the West, then around the world. With nationalism came the creation of mass systems of education, one of whose goals was to instill active loyalty to state and nation. And what better way to do this than to present history in terms of a national success story (sometimes bolstered by courses in national literature as well). History came to revolve around the nation state, its origins, its successful struggles against adversity, its heroes and shining moments. Here was a powerful basis for deciding what facts should be emphasized and what spin should be put upon the past. One of the reasons many people become upset by evidence that many students don't know standard facts about American history is that the ignorance calls both identity and loyalty into question. Particularly in times of high immigration, like the 1900s and again today, American educators have been pressed to make sure that a common body of national historical knowledge, and a common appreciation for the historical roots of national greatness, organize their teaching objectives.

Here too, many actual historians worry about an oversimple justification for history. They note that nations (including our own) have bad pasts as well as good ones, and believe we might learn more from mistakes (like the treatment of minority races) than from successes. They note that the nationalist enthusiasm for history, in many countries, has encouraged outright myths or "invented traditions," in which an imaginary past is used to justify particular standards in the present day. Of course, contemporary uses of history for identity are not confined to the nation state. Companies, trade unions, ethnic groups all have their versions of history, designed to provide identity by emphasizing common successes and/or sufferings in the past, often with some of the same dangers of oversimplification attached. Even family values have a stake in historical identity, with images of tightly knit families in the past used to guide and cajole familes in the present (with nostalgic models that, as most family historians would note, are often quite inaccurate).

In sum, history has always been a powerful subject, even though it can degenerate into mindless memorization of facts. It continues to be a vital source of group identity and pride. History as moral example is often harnessed to identity needs by providing cases studies of heroic action to serve as models for contemporary youth. In service of the nation state, identity history provides the clearest reason history is such a widely taught subject in schools today. The goal of understanding can also concentrate on a sense of analogy, on a belief that certain kinds of experiences recur, if not literally then in broad outline, such that knowledge of the past can inform and guide reactions to an otherwise uncertain present. It is almost impossible not to think in terms of analogy—trying to make sense of a present dilemma by looking for ways it resembles something encountered before. And as we have seen, policymakers often build arguments on historical analogies. Yet we have also seen that many historians are uncomfortable both with identity history (particularly the nationalist variety) and with analogy and its claim that the past repeats. Their version of historical thinking, not brand new but articulated with increasing care in the past twenty years, goes beyond the conventional staples, while incorporating some of their elements.

❖ History as a Habit of Mind

Historical thinking, in this final version, involves a mixture of precise skills and more general habits of mind. Skills include learning to assess evidence, or what historians call "primary sources," produced for various purposes in the past by various kinds of people. To properly develop a historical argument, one has to combine different kinds of evidence (images, films, and statistics as well as texts) and sort out issues of reliability, bias, and representativeness—skills that can be crucial for other kinds of research tasks, work, and citizenship obligations. Historians are becoming increasingly practiced in training students to find and handle evidence (including, now, evidence from the Internet).

History students must also learn to assess conflicting interpretations—another key aspect of doing history that can extend to other tasks in life. Historians disagree a lot, and over time advance knowledge through debate. Historical debates provide an opportunity to test different arguments according to how well they uncover and use evidence. More broadly, learning how to jump into a debate and sort out the ingredients, in order to mount one's own argument, is a challenging opportunity to develop important critical skills. The capacity can be particularly important in dealing objectively with histories advanced to support identity claims, including the claims of national leaders proffering their own understandings of the nation's past. Many historians would add that the discipline encourages good writing and communication skills and the ability to develop cogent arguments, though other subjects contribute as well.

❖ History as an Exploration in Change

But the central modern claim about the nature and importance of historical thinking centers on change—or, more properly, on change and continuity. History is really the record of change, and its study provides the tools that offer the greatest promise for understanding change. There are several points here.

First, history provides a laboratory of human experience, with all sorts of examples of change, so learning history develops skills in evaluating the magnitude of change. We're constantly bombarded with claims of unprecedented change, or revolutionary this-or-that, and we need the perspective that history provides to help sort this out. Not all changes are fundamental; some confirm established directions, with a new twist or two; some really do alter basic frameworks. Only practice with the past provides any chance of sorting out these levels. There are some very basic steps involved, which stand out only if we break historical thinking down. To understand levels of change, for example, one needs a clear baseline—the situation before major change began—and an understanding of timing—when the change started, how rapidly it proceeded, and when it became established as an ongoing trend. Knowing what historical thinking consists of helps us do this better and faster, along with repeated experience in actual case studies.

Explorations of causation comprise the second facet of core historical analysis, which again provides practice for assessing types of change occurring around us today. Sometimes fairly recent history will provide an adequate context to explain change, but often we need to look farther back to identify causes. Here, factual knowledge combines with analytical ability honed by experience. Developments that trigger change—explaining what change occurs when it does—will often differ from those that really set up change and its direction. Once again, these skills can be developed by looking at historical case studies. The same exercises show how the present emerges from the past, by exploring patterns of change that led up to current behaviors. When and why, for example, did Americans begin to avoid voting in elections, a change from both the 19th century and the 1930s? Answering this question of causation helps provide a handle on an important current phenomenon, and may offer insight into ways to change behavior yet again, should this be desired. If one doesn't know why voting habits changed, it's hard to understand modern American politics.

Dealing with change can often involve comparison. While voter turnout in both the United States and western Europe has dropped in recent decades, the American plunge began earlier and went farther. Adding comparison to the discussion of causes will deepen understanding.

Finally—and here too comparison can often enter in—change is rarely complete. It normally combines with substantial continuity. In the 1950s and 1960s, for example, married women in western Europe and the United States began to enter the formal labor force in record numbers, a huge change for them and their families alike. But they often took jobs that were distinctively feminine and believed that in fact they should not be working at all, that caring for their families should come first. Change here combined with older values in ways that could be personally painful. On a larger scale, many key issues in the world today involve societies reacting to similar forces for change—like global consumer products—in quite different ways based on different continuities from different prior traditions. Distinctive historical identities confront change in predictably varied fashion.

The analytical challenge in sorting all this out is considerable, but it is the only way to make sense of what has happened in the past and how the past leads to the present. Assessing magnitude, dealing with causation, comparing different reactions to a common change, and pulling in continuity is crucial to understanding how the past has evolved—even the remote past. These skills give meaning to otherwise disconnected facts, requiring that they be put together and assessed in ways that explore change. And they highlight how current and possibly future patterns relate to developments in the past, emerging from them in combinations of change and continuity. Dealing with change is the reason that oversimple reliance on history for identity falls short, because identities are not constant; and also the reason that unsubtle analogies also fail, again because contexts shift too much for analogies to be accurate guides.

This focus on change, as the essence of historical thinking, applies to a wide range, for history's subject matter is hardly confined to politics or diplomacy alone. We need historical analysis to understand why and how political behaviors change, or why different troublespots emerge in world diplomacy. But we also need historical perspective closer to home, concerning some very basic human activities. Why do many Americans hesitate to take children to funerals or to discuss death with them, when a hundred years ago children and death were closely associated? When and why did smiling become so important in Western culture (one historian has traced this one back to the 18th century and to new products for tooth care)? Why do we worry so much about being bored (the language for identifying boredom is only about 200 years old)? Fundamental aspects of what we might view as human nature are actually open to periodic change, which again means that we understand ourselves only by thinking historically—finding the necessary fact about change but also knowing how to use them. The core of historical thinking starts with realizing that the past is different from the present, often in some unexpected ways, but also that the present emerged from the past through changes that we can probe. Thinking historically in this basic sense is not only exciting, but also liberating. The opportunity is not only guidance in not repeating the past, but also in grasping how things came to be as they are.

Why Study History?

People live in the present. They plan for and worry about the future. History, however, is the study of the past. Given all the demands that press in from living in the present and anticipating what is yet to come, why bother with what has been? Given all the desirable and available branches of knowledge, why insist— as most American educational programs do—on studying history? And why urge many students to study even more history than they are required to?

Any subject of study needs justification: its advocates must explain why it is worth attention. Most widely accepted subjects—and history is certainly one of them—attract some people who simply like the information and modes of thought involved. But audiences less spontaneously drawn to the subject and more doubtful about why to bother need to know what the purpose is.

Historians do not perform heart transplants, improve highway design, or arrest criminals. In a society that quite correctly expects education to serve useful purposes, the functions of history can seem more difficult to define than those of engineering or medicine. History is in fact very useful, actually indispensable, but the products of historical study are less tangible, sometimes less immediate, than those that stem from some other disciplines.

In the past, history has been justified for reasons we would no longer accept. For instance, one of the reasons history holds its place in current education is because earlier leaders believed that a knowledge of certain historical facts helped distinguish the educated from the uneducated; the person who could reel off the date of the Norman conquest of England (1066) or the name of the person who came up with the theory of evolution at about the same time that Darwin did (Wallace) was deemed superior—a better candidate for law school or even a business promotion. Knowledge of historical facts has been used as a screening device in many societies, from China to the United States, and the habit is still with us to some extent. Unfortunately, this use can encourage mindless memorization—a real but not very appealing aspect of the discipline.

History should be studied because it is essential to individuals and to society, and because it harbors beauty. There are many ways to discuss the real functions of the subject—as there are many different historical talents and many different paths to historical meaning. All definitions of history's utility, however, rely on two fundamental facts.

❖ History Helps Us Understand Peoples and Societies

In the first place, history offers a storehouse of information about how people and societies behave. Understanding the operations of people and societies is difficult, though a number of disciplines make the attempt. An exclusive reliance on current data would needlessly handicap our efforts. How can we evaluate war if the nation is at peace—unless we use historical materials? How can we understand genius, the influence of technological innovation, or the role that beliefs play in shaping family life, if we don't use what we know about experiences in the past? Some social scientists attempt to formulate laws or theories about human behavior. But even these recourses depend on historical information, except for in limited, often artificial cases in which experiments can be devised to determine how people act. Major aspects of a society's operation, like mass elections, missionary activities, or military alliances, cannot be set up as precise experiments. Consequently, history must serve, however imperfectly, as our laboratory, and data from the past must serve as our most vital evidence in the unavoidable quest to figure out why our complex species behaves as it does in societal settings. This, fundamentally, is why we cannot stay away from history: it offers the only extensive evidential base for the contemplation and analysis of how societies function, and people need to have some sense of how societies function simply to run their own lives.

❖ History Explains How the Present Emerged from the Past

The second reason history is inescapable as a subject of serious study follows closely on the first. The past causes the present, and so the future. Any time we try to know why something happened—whether a shift in political party dominance in the American Congress, a major change in the teenage suicide rate, or a war in the Balkans or the Middle East—we have to look for factors that took shape earlier. Sometimes fairly recent history will suffice to explain a major development, but often we need to look further back to identify the causes of change. Only through studying history can we grasp how things change; only through history can we begin to comprehend the factors that cause change; and only through history can we understand what elements of an institution or a society persist despite change.

The importance of history in explaining and understanding change in human behavior is no mere abstraction. Take an important human phenomenon such as alcoholism. Through biological experiments scientists have identified specific genes that seem to cause a proclivity toward alcohol addiction in some individuals. This is a notable advance. But alcoholism, as a social reality, has a history: rates of alcoholism have risen and fallen, and they have varied from one group to the next. Attitudes and policies about alcoholism have also changed and varied. History is indispensable to understanding why such changes occur. And in many ways historical analysis is a more challenging kind of exploration than genetic experimentation. Historians have in fact greatly contributed in recent decades to our understanding of trends (or patterns of change) in alcoholism and to our grasp of the dimensions of addiction as an evolving social problem.

One of the leading concerns of contemporary American politics is low voter turnout, even for major elections. A historical analysis of changes in voter turnout can help us begin to understand the problem we face today. What were turnouts in the past? When did the decline set in? Once we determine when the trend began, we can try to identify which of the factors present at the time combined to set the trend in motion. Do the same factors sustain the trend still, or are there new ingredients that have contributed to it in more recent decades? A purely contemporary analysis may shed some light on the problem, but a historical assessment is clearly fundamental—and essential for anyone concerned about American political health today.

Only history can provide such extensive materials to study the human condition. It also focuses attention on the complex processes of social change, including the factors that are causing change around us today. Here, at base, are the two related reasons many people become enthralled with the examination of the past and why our society requires and encourages the study of history as a major subject in the schools.

These two fundamental reasons for studying history underlie more specific and quite diverse uses of history in our own lives. History well told is beautiful. Many of the historians who most appeal to the general reading public know the importance of dramatic and skillful writing—as well as of accuracy. Biography and military history appeal in part because of the tales they contain. History as art and entertainment serves a real purpose, on aesthetic grounds but also on the level of human understanding. Stories well done are stories that reveal how people and societies have actually functioned, and they prompt thoughts about the human experience in other times and places. The same aesthetic and humanistic goals inspire people to immerse themselves in efforts to reconstruct quite remote pasts, far removed from immediate, present-day utility. Exploring what historians sometimes call the "pastness of the past"—the ways people in distant ages constructed their lives—involves a sense of beauty and excitement, and ultimately another perspective on human life and society.

❖ History Contributes to Understanding

History also provides a terrain for moral contemplation. Studying the stories of individuals and situations in the past allows a student of history to test his or her own moral sense, and to hone it against some of the real complexities individuals have faced in difficult settings. People who have weathered adversity not just in some work of fiction, but in real, historical circumstances can provide inspiration. "History teaching by example" is one phrase that describes this use of a study of the past—a study not only of certifiable heroes, the great men and women of history who successfully worked through moral dilemmas, but also of more ordinary people who provide lessons in courage, diligence, or constructive protest.

History also helps provide identity, and this is unquestionably one of the reasons all modern nations encourage its teaching in some form. Historical data include evidence about how families, groups, institutions, and whole countries were formed and about how they have evolved while retaining cohesion. For many Americans, studying the history of one's own family is the most obvious use of history, for it provides facts about genealogy and (at a slightly more complex level) a basis for understanding how the family has interacted with larger historical change. Family identity is established and confirmed. Many institutions, businesses, communities, and social units, such as ethnic groups in the United States, use history for similar identity purposes. Merely defining the group in the present pales against the possibility of forming an identity based on a rich past. And of course nations use identity history as well—and sometimes abuse it. Histories that tell the national story, emphasizing distinctive features of the national experience, are meant to drive home an understanding of national values and a commitment to national loyalty.

A study of history is essential for good citizenship. This is the most common justification for the place of history in school curricula. Sometimes advocates of citizenship history hope merely to promote national identity and loyalty through a history spiced by vivid stories and lessons in individual success and morality. But the importance of history for citizenship goes beyond this narrow goal and can even challenge it at some points.

History that lays the foundation for genuine citizenship returns, in one sense, to the essential uses of the study of the past. History provides data about the emergence of national institutions, problems, and values—it's the only significant storehouse of such data available. It offers evidence also about how nations have interacted with other societies, providing international and comparative perspectives essential for responsible citizenship. Further, studying history helps us understand how recent, current, and prospective changes that affect the lives of citizens are emerging or may emerge and what causes are involved. More important, studying history encourages habits of mind that are vital for responsible public behavior, whether as a national or community leader, an informed voter, a petitioner, or a simple observer.

❖ History Teaches Skills for Living

What does a well-trained student of history, schooled to work on past materials and on case studies in social change, learn how to do? The list is manageable, but it contains several overlapping categories.

The Ability to Assess Evidence. The study of history builds experience in dealing with and assessing various kinds of evidence—the sorts of evidence historians use in shaping the most accurate pictures of the past that they can. Learning how to interpret the statements of past political leaders—one kind of evidence—helps form the capacity to distinguish between the objective and the self-serving among statements made by present-day political leaders. Learning how to combine different kinds of evidence—public statements, private records, numerical data, visual materials—develops the ability to make coherent arguments based on a variety of data. This skill can also be applied to information encountered in everyday life.

The Ability to Assess Conflicting Interpretations. Learning history means gaining some skill in sorting through diverse, often conflicting interpretations. Understanding how societies work—the central goal of historical study—is inherently imprecise, and the same certainly holds true for understanding what is going on in the present day. Learning how to identify and evaluate conflicting interpretations is an essential citizenship skill for which history, as an often-contested laboratory of human experience, provides training. This is one area in which the full benefits of historical study sometimes clash with the narrower uses of the past to construct identity. Experience in examining past situations provides a constructively critical sense that can be applied to partisan claims about the glories of national or group identity. The study of history in no sense undermines loyalty or commitment, but it does teach the need for assessing arguments, and it provides opportunities to engage in debate and achieve perspective.

Experience in Assessing Past Examples of Change. Experience in assessing past examples of change is vital to understanding change in society today—it's an essential skill in what we are regularly told is our "ever-changing world." Analysis of change means developing some capacity for determining the magnitude and significance of change, for some changes are more fundamental than others. Comparing particular changes to relevant examples from the past helps students of history develop this capacity. The ability to identify the continuities that always accompany even the most dramatic changes also comes from studying history, as does the skill to determine probable causes of change. Learning history helps one figure out, for example, if one main factor—such as a technological innovation or some deliberate new policy—accounts for a change or whether, as is more commonly the case, a number of factors combine to generate the actual change that occurs.

Historical study, in sum, is crucial to the promotion of that elusive creature, the well-informed citizen. It provides basic factual information about the background of our political institutions and about the values and problems that affect our social well-being. It also contributes to our capacity to use evidence, assess interpretations, and analyze change and continuities. No one can ever quite deal with the present as the historian deals with the past—we lack the perspective for this feat; but we can move in this direction by applying historical habits of mind, and we will function as better citizens in the process.

❖ History in the Workplace

History is also useful for work. Its study helps create good businesspeople, professionals, and political leaders. The number of explicit professional jobs for historians is considerable, but most people who study history do not become professional historians. Professional historians teach at various levels, work in museums and media centers, do historical research for businesses or public agencies, or participate in the growing number of historical consultancies. These categories are important—indeed vital—to keep the basic enterprise of history going, but most people who study history use their training for broader professional purposes.

Students of history find their experience directly relevant to jobs in a variety of careers as well as to further study in fields like law and public administration. Employers often deliberately seek students with the kinds of capacities historical study promotes. The reasons are not hard to identify: students of history acquire, by studying different phases of the past and different societies in the past, a broad perspective that gives them the range and flexibility required in many work situations. They develop research skills, the ability to find and evaluate sources of information, and the means to identify and evaluate diverse interpretations. Work in history also improves basic writing and speaking skills and is directly relevant to many of the analytical requirements in the public and private sectors, where the capacity to identify, assess, and explain trends is essential.

Historical study is unquestionably an asset for a variety of work and professional situations, even though it does not, for most students, lead as directly to a particular job slot, as do some technical fields. But history particularly prepares students for the long haul in their careers, its qualities helping adaptation and advancement beyond entry-level employment. There is no denying that in our society many people who are drawn to historical study worry about relevance. In our changing economy, there is concern about job futures in most fields. Historical training is not, however, an indulgence; it applies directly to many careers and can clearly help us in our working lives.

❖ What Kind of History?

The question of why we should study history entails several subsidiary issues about what kind of history should be studied. Historians and the general public alike can generate a lot of heat about what specific history courses should appear in what part of the curriculum. Many of the benefits of history derive from various kinds of history, whether local or national or focused on one culture or the world. Gripping instances of history as storytelling, as moral example, and as analysis come from all sorts of settings. The most intense debates about what history should cover occur in relation to identity history and the attempt to argue that knowledge of certain historical facts marks one as an educated person. Some people feel that in order to become good citizens students must learn to recite the preamble of the American Constitution or be able to identify Thomas Edison—though many historians would dissent from an unduly long list of factual obligations. Correspondingly, some feminists, eager to use history as part of their struggle, want to make sure that students know the names of key past leaders such as Susan B. Anthony. The range of possible survey and memorization chores is considerable— one reason that history texts are often quite long.

There is a fundamental tension in teaching and learning history between covering facts and developing historical habits of mind. Because history provides an immediate background to our own life and age, it is highly desirable to learn about forces that arose in the past and continue to affect the modern world. This type of knowledge requires some attention to comprehending the development of national institutions and trends. It also demands some historical understanding of key forces in the wider world. The ongoing tension between Christianity and Islam, for instance, requires some knowledge of patterns that took shape over 12 centuries ago. Indeed, the pressing need to learn about issues of importance throughout the world is the basic reason that world history has been gaining ground in American curriculums. Historical habits of mind are enriched when we learn to compare different patterns of historical development, which means some study of other national traditions and civilizations.

The key to developing historical habits of mind, however, is having repeated experience in historical inquiry. Such experience should involve a variety of materials and a diversity of analytical problems. Facts are essential in this process, for historical analysis depends on data, but it does not matter whether these facts come from local, national, or world history—although it's most useful to study a range of settings. What matters is learning how to assess different magnitudes of historical change, different examples of conflicting interpretations, and multiple kinds of evidence. Developing the ability to repeat fundamental thinking habits through increasingly complex exercises is essential. Historical processes and institutions that are deemed especially important to specific curriculums can, of course, be used to teach historical inquiry. Appropriate balance is the obvious goal, with an insistence on factual knowledge not allowed to overshadow the need to develop historical habits of mind.

Exposure to certain essential historical episodes and experience in historical inquiry are crucial to any program of historical study, but they require supplement. No program can be fully functional if it does not allow for whimsy and individual taste. Pursuing particular stories or types of problems, simply because they tickle the fancy, contributes to a rounded intellectual life. Similarly, no program in history is complete unless it provides some understanding of the ongoing role of historical inquiry in expanding our knowledge of the past and, with it, of human and social behavior. The past two decades have seen a genuine explosion of historical information and analysis, as additional facets of human behavior have been subjected to research and interpretation. And there is every sign that historians are continuing to expand our understanding of the past. It's clear that the discipline of history is a source of innovation and not merely a framework for repeated renderings of established data and familiar stories.

Why study history? The answer is because we virtually must, to gain access to the laboratory of human experience. When we study it reasonably well, and so acquire some usable habits of mind, as well as some basic data about the forces that affect our own lives, we emerge with relevant skills and an enhanced capacity for informed citizenship, critical thinking, and simple awareness. The uses of history are varied. Studying history can help us develop some literally "salable" skills, but its study must not be pinned down to the narrowest utilitarianism. Some history— that confined to personal recollections about changes and continuities in the immediate environment—is essential to function beyond childhood. Some history depends on personal taste, where one finds beauty, the joy of discovery, or intellectual challenge. Between the inescapable minimum and the pleasure of deep commitment comes the history that, through cumulative skill in interpreting the unfolding human record, provides a real grasp of how the world works.

Further Reading

Cannadine, David, Ed. *What Is History Now?* New York: Palgrave Macmillan, 2002.

Holt, Thomas C. *Thinking Historically: Narrative, Imagination, and Understanding*. New York: College Entrance Examination Board, 1990.

Schulz, Constance et al. *Careers for Students of History*. Washington, D.C.: American Historical Association, 2002.

Hexter, J. H. *The History Primer*. New York: Basic Books, 1971.

Gagnon, Paul, ed. *Historical Literacy*. New York: MacMillan, 1989.

Gustafson, Melanie. *Becoming a Historian, 2003 Edition*. Washington, D.C.: American Historical Association, 2003.

Lowenthal, David. *The Heritage Crusade and the Spoils of History*. New York: Cambridge University Press, 1998.

Lowenthal, David. *The Past is a Foreign Country*. New York: Cambridge University Press, 1985.

Oakeshott, Michael. *On History*. Totowa, N.J.: Barnes and Noble, 1983.

Stearns, Peter N. *Meaning over Memory: Recasting the Teaching of History and Culture*. Chapel Hill: University of North Carolina Press, 1993.

Stearns, Peter N., Peter Seixas, and Samuel S. Wineburg, Eds. *Knowing, Teaching, and Learning History: National and International Perspectives*. New York: New York University Press, 2000.

Wineburg, Sam. *Historical Thinking and Other Unnatural Acts*. Philadlphia: Temple University Press, 2001